This book is dedicated to the memory of

Mary Anne Hyche.

Her faith and courage were an inspiration to all who knew her,

especially her husband, John, and their children, John and Katie.

Mary Anne's life was an example for all who loved her that our lives

should be guided and inspired by a love of God.

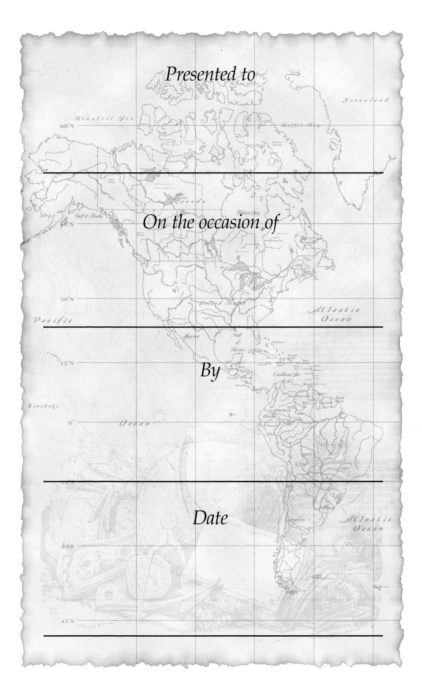

Presented to

_____

On the occasion of

_____

By

_____

Date

_____

Written by
Elaine Murray Stone

Regina
Press

Nihil Obstat: Reverend Robert O. Morrissey, J.C.D.
Censor librorum
June 16, 2003

Imprimatur: Most Reverend William Murphy
Bishop of Rockville Centre
June 23, 2003

THE REGINA PRESS
10 Hub Drive
Melville, New York 11747

Special thanks to Mr. Brian Broughton for his assistance with this project.

Artwork © Copyright 2004 by Quadriga, New York with the exception of:
Page 56 — *Blessed Marie Guyard Martin*, Urslines of Chatham, Chatham, ON
Page 68 — Sister Saint-Rene (Lachance), C.N.D., *Marguerite Bourgeoys at the first school of Ville-Marie* (1904), Marguerite Bourgeoys Museum, Montreal, QC
Page 73 — *St. Marguerite d'Youville*, Centre Marguerite-d'Youville, Montreal, QC
Page 79 — *Blessed Alfred Bessette*, Saint Joseph's Oratory of Mount Royal, Montreal, QC
Page 92 — Christina Miller. *Pierre Toussaint*, iconfusion@earthlink.net

If any required credits have been omitted, it is unintentional, and the publisher will correct any omissions in future reprints.

Printed in Hong Kong.

ISBN: 0-88271-349-3

Table of Contents

Canada

United States

Introduction

Most Catholics are familiar with saints such as St. Augustine, St. Francis of Assisi, and St. Patrick. They lived and died in the Old World long before Christopher Columbus discovered America. Soon after the Nina, Pinta, and the Santa Maria arrived from Spain, many missionaries came from Europe to convert the indigenous peoples. Not as well known to most readers are the saints of the New World: North, South, and Central America, plus the islands of the West Indies. This book tells their stories.

Priest, friars, and nuns crossed the wide Atlantic, most of them landing in the northern areas of South America. They were burning with desire to bring the joy and love of Christ to those who had never heard of Our Lord.

The very first Mass in the present United States was celebrated in 1565 at St. Augustine, Florida. Soon after, Franciscan friars from Spain built missions all along the east coast of Florida. Later, other Franciscans, such as Blessed Junípero Serra, built the famous missions of California.

In the sixteenth and seventeenth centuries, French missionaries ventured into the wilds of Canada, preaching the good news about Jesus, and founded schools and hospitals. Many brave priests, such as St. Isaac Jogues and his companions, were martyred for their faith. Then, French nuns arrived to build convents, missions, and schools in Canada and in states such as Indiana, Missouri, Mississippi, and Louisiana.

There are saints who were actually born in the New World, among them St. Juan Diego of Mexico, St. Rose of Lima, and St. Elizabeth Ann Seton of New York City. Some saints even lived in modern times. Best known are the "leper saint," Blessed Joseph de Veuster (Father Damien), St. Frances Cabrini, the foundress of great hospitals in New York and Chicago; Blessed Miguel Pro, who was martyred in Mexico; and St. Katherine Drexel, who was just recently canonized.

I have written these short biographies of men and women saints of the Americas to make them better known to a wider audience. Dedicated and brave, they serve as an inspiration to all of us who live in the Americas.

Elaine Murray Stone

Mexico

St. Juan Diego
Our Lady of Guadalupe
1474-1548

*J*uan Diego was born in Mexico in 1474. In 1521, Hernado Cortez conquered the Aztecs and the Spaniards took over Mexico. Soon Franciscan and Dominican friars came from Spain to convert the Mexicans. Juan was one of the first. He gave up his cruel Aztec gods and became a Catholic.

On the feast of the Immaculate Conception, Juan set out to attend Mass in a nearby town. As he passed Tepeyac Hill he heard many birds singing. Then a sweet voice called, "Juan, Juan. Come up here. I have something to tell you."

Juan might have walked on, but the lady's voice grew louder and more insistent. Finally, curious, Juan climbed the hill. At the top stood a beautiful young woman with brown skin and black hair, just like his. The apparition was dressed in pink; a blue cape dotted with gold stars fell over her hair to the ground.

To Juan's astonishment, the vision said, "I am the Virgin Mary. I desire that a church be built here in my honor. Go to Mexico City and tell the bishop what you have seen and heard."

Juan was filled with fear, but he obeyed the beautiful lady and struck out for the capital city. When he arrived at the bishop's residence, the doorkeeper would not let him in. Juan didn't give up. He tried and tried. Finally, he was admitted to Bishop Juan de Zumárraga's residence. Juan gave the bishop the lady's message.

After hearing more of Juan's strange story, the bishop sent him away, saying, "Ask your lady for a sign. Then I will fulfill her request."

Juan hurried home, where he tended to his sick uncle. Then he made three more visits to Tepeyac Hill. Once again, on December 12, 1531, Juan climbed the hill. He saw the beautiful lady and gave her the bishop's message.

The lady ordered the bewildered Indian to gather roses. He protested, "It is winter. How can roses bloom here in the cold?" She repeated her command, and two red rosebushes appeared. Juan removed his cloak and filled it with the miraculous roses. With the bright red roses tied up in his cloak, Juan hurried off to show Bishop Zumárraga.

"Do you have a sign?" asked the unbelieving bishop. Saying nothing, Juan opened his cloak and dozens of fresh roses fell to the floor, but the bishop and other clergy weren't admiring the flowers. Rather, they stared in wonder at Juan's cloak. On it was a picture of the Virgin Mary, just as he had described her. They fell to their knees in adoration.

The bishop was quick to honor the Virgin Mary's request. A chapel was built in only two weeks at Tepeyac Hill. Juan's cloak with the painting was hung above the altar, and the chapel quickly became a place of pilgrimage. Many miracles of healing took place there. The Indians were pleased that the holy Virgin had honored them this way. By 1538, five million Mexicans were converted and baptized. In time, the entire population became Catholic.

In 1709, a great basilica was built to replace the chapel. Millions of pilgrims have visited it to see the representation of the Virgin Mary.

Blessed Miguel Pro
Mexican Martyr
1891-1927

*T*he young priest knelt with his arms outstretched to form a cross. As the firing-squad soldiers cocked their weapons, the condemned man shouted, "Long live Christ the King!" Then the officer gave the command, the guns fired, and the priest fell dead.

Who was this priest? And why was he executed?

Miguel Augustin Pro was born in Guadalupe, Mexico, on January 13, 1891. His father, also named Miguel Pro, was head engineer at a silver mine. He married Josefa Suarez and had ten children. Miguel was their first.

Migueltio, as he was called, was a handful: over-active and mischievous. One time he climbed out the window to a ledge three floors above the street. At the last second his nurse pulled him to safety. In his teens he played many practical jokes, often embarrassing his parents.

After his sister, Conception, entered a cloistered

convent, Miguel became serious. He applied for admission to the Jesuit order. Having heard of the young candidate's tricks, the rector played one on Miguel. The rector let Miguel wait an hour while he read the newspaper from front to back. Then the Jesuit recommended Miguel return the next day, at which time the rector was too busy writing to speak to him.

Eventually, Miguel was admitted to the Jesuit novitiate in Michoacan on August 11, 1911. He couldn't have chosen a worse time. In 1910, an anti-Catholic revolution began throughout Mexico. Churches were boarded up; priests and Religious went into hiding.

For their safety the novitiate was closed. The young novices dressed as peasants, and then traveled by train to California. Eventually, Miguel sailed to Europe, where he continued his education in Spain. He was ordained to the priesthood in Belgium on August 31, 1925. Because it was so far from Mexico, his parents were unable to attend.

His European superiors, unaware how serious the persecution of Catholic priests had become in Mexico, sent Father Pro there to begin his priestly duties. By then Catholic clergy were not allowed to say Mass, dispense the sacraments, or wear clerical collars.

Father Pro and his two Religious brothers joined a subversive organization, the National League for the Defense of Religious Rights. Mexicans were forbidden to be married in a church or have their babies baptized. Priests had to wear ordinary clothes and hide underground from the police. That was when Father Pro's playfulness came in handy.

The young priest wore all sorts of disguises. He dressed as a peasant or a laborer. Sometimes he pretended to be a student bicycling around the city. He put consecrated hosts under his clothes, and said Mass in hiding. The faithful Mexicans never gave him away.

Father Pro also found ways to hear confessions, marry young couples, and even prepare children for First Communion.

Just one time, Father Pro was caught and put in jail. His two Religious brothers were also imprisoned. The jailer tried to trap Father Pro by asking, "Which one of you will be saying Mass for the prisoners? Which one of you is the priest?"

Laughing, Father Pro replied, "Oh, I'm not a priest. You are confused; my name is 'Pro'." Pro is a Mexican word for priest (presbyterio).

Another time, a suspicious policeman followed Father Pro for blocks. Turning a corner, he saw a young woman he knew. He put his arm around her shoulders. Seeing what looked like a happy young couple, the policeman dropped his pursuit.

Father Pro's luck finally ran out. In 1912, a bomb was thrown at the car of the president–elect of Mexico. Tossed from another automobile, it was discovered that the car had originally belonged to Father Pro's brother. All three of the Pro brothers were arrested and accused of the assassination attempt on General Alvaro Obregon.

Without a trial or any witnesses, Father Pro was sentenced to death. An attempt to save his life came too late. Father Pro's sister arrived at the prison with a reprieve for her accused brother. The jailer refused to admit her. He kept the prison gate locked until after she heard the shots from the firing squad.

The vain president, Plutarco Calles, had invited newsmen and photographers to attend the execution. This backfired. When the populace read the sad story and saw the gruesome photos of the dead young priest, they went wild. Thousands poured into the streets for Father Pro's funeral. Hundreds of cars were in the procession.

Many people cried and threw flowers on the casket.

Everyone wanted to express grief, even if it angered the president. Just days after Father Pro's execution, several miracles took place. They were attributed to the murdered young priest. Many who prayed to him were healed or had other requests answered.

In 1952, Father Pro's Cause was begun. He was beatified on September 25, 1988, by Pope John Paul II in Rome. His feast day is November 23.

Central America and Caribbean

St. Pedro de San Jose Betancur
St. Francis of the Americas
1619-1667

*P*edro de San Jose Betancur was the first saint to be canonized in Central America. He was born in the Canary Islands off Spain in 1619. Pedro came from a poor family and received little education. He worked as a shepherd, which might have been his lifelong career, but while sitting out on the hills with his sheep, he dreamed of becoming a missionary in the New World.

In 1651, he realized his dream, sailing to Guatemala in Central America. By then thirty-one years old, Pedro began working among the poor of the capital, Guatemala City. Hoping to become a priest, Pedro entered the Jesuit seminary, but his lack of education kept him from graduating, or being ordained. Instead, he took the vows of a Franciscan tertiary.

Known as Hermano Pedro (Brother Peter), he began his charitable work by starting a hospital for the poor, called Our Lady of Bethlehem. To supply it with dedicated workers, he founded two religious orders called the Bethlemite Congregation. At one time there were five hundred Bethlemite brothers, but today there are only ten. However, still today the Bethlemite Sisters care for the sick and poor in thirteen countries.

To raise money for his hospitals, schools, and chapels, Brother Peter walked through the city's wealthy districts ringing a silver bell as he begged for alms for the sick and poor.

Brother Peter is credited with starting the Christmas Eve custom of "Posadas." People dress in costumes like those of Mary and Joseph. They walk through town knocking on doors and asking for a place to sleep. This custom eventually spread throughout Latin America.

Brother Peter died on April 25, 1667. The whole city mourned the saintly man's passing. They compared him to St. Francis of Assisi, who also helped the poor.

It became a custom for people to knock on his tomb when praying for health or help. This tradition continued into modern times, often resulting in miracles. Accordingly, two miracles required for Brother Peter's beatification and canonization were easy to find.

Brother Peter continued to be an inspiration to the common people of Guatemala, of whom sixty percent are Indians and Mayans. For three and a half centuries that inspiration grew. The gentle brother was beatified on June 22, 1980, by Pope John Paul II.

From 1960 to 1996, Guatemala was torn by a cruel civil war. During it, two hundred thousand people died. The arrival of Pope John Paul II to canonize their saint brought great joy to the Guatemalan Catholics. They built a road covered with sand and flowers for the Pope's arrival on July 29, 2002. The three-hour ceremony took place at Guatemala City's racetrack, the largest open area. Half a million people attended the canonization on July 30.

Speaking from a raised platform, Pope John Paul said of the saintly brother: "Hermano Pedro was a man of deep faith and prayer. In Christ he found the strength to practice mercy heroically among the poorest and most deprived. This new saint personifies a heritage that must not be lost for the sake of a world filled with suffering people." A high point of the Mass was the ringing of St. Peter's little silver bell throughout the reading of his biography. It was the same ancient bell the humble saint rang while begging for alms.

Many young people wore T-shirts printed with the new saint's image. After praying all night in a soccer stadium, they walked five miles to attend the canonization.

Guatemalans, young and old, are proud to be the first in Central America to have a native saint, Pedro de San Jose Betancur.

St. Anthony Mary Claret
Archbishop of Cuba and
Founder of the Claretians
1807-1870

Anthony was the fifth child of Juan and Josefina Claret, who owned a small weaving factory. During his teens, Anthony learned the art of weaving, and might have remained in the textile business except for his desire to become a priest.

Although quite strong-willed during his childhood, this future saint worked hard to overcome his obstinate nature.

Anthony was born in Vallent, Spain, on Christmas Eve 1807. With so many brothers and sisters, he enjoyed a happy childhood. The youngster was so deeply devoted to the Mother of God, he took her name, Mary, at his confirmation.

Although Anthony had always wanted to become a priest, he didn't enter the seminary until he was twenty-seven. Before that he started a textile factory in Barcelona. He also studied Latin with a tutor in preparation for someday entering the priesthood. This he finally did

when he entered the seminary at Vich.

Following his ordination on June 13, 1835, Anthony, now Father Claret, went to Rome, planning to join the Society of Jesus. Soon after entering the Jesuit novitiate, he became lame, unable to walk. No doctor could discover a cause for his disability. However, the day he left the Jesuits, Father Claret was instantly healed. Obviously, the Jesuit order was not meant for him.

Father Claret next offered himself as a missionary. He was first sent to the Canary Islands off the northwest coast of Africa. After a fruitful fifteen months there, Father Claret returned to Spain, where he soon discovered his true vocation.

Father Claret had two great talents: one as a preacher, the other as a teacher of the catechism. Over the course of his life, Father Claret preached twenty-five thousand sermons, and wrote one hundred forty books, most of them short and long catechisms. He also was the first author to add illustrations to religious books for children. Called the greatest catechist of the nineteenth century, he gradually recognized a great need for more priests able to conduct missions. There was no better way to turn people's hearts to God.

In 1849, with five other young priests, Father Claret founded the Missionary Sons of the Immaculate Heart of Mary. Their main work was preaching missions. Such priests became known as "Claretians" in honor of their esteemed founder, Father Claret.

That same year, Father Claret was appointed archbishop of Cuba. Arriving at the West Indian island, he discovered the Catholic Church there in great disarray. To change the situation, he visited every church and mission on the island.

Now Archbishop Claret, he confirmed thousands of children, and married nine thousand couples who had been living in sin. He reopened Cuba's only seminary, founded two religious orders, and started a ranch for homeless boys.

Unfortunately, all these changes created many enemies for the archbishop. One day he was attacked by a would-be assassin. The future saint received several knife wounds, one cutting the entire side of his face.

Just as all was improving in Cuba, the queen of Spain called him home. Queen Isabella II wanted Archbishop Claret to become her personal confessor. Once in Madrid, Archbishop Claret found he was not meant for life at the Spanish court. There was too much intrigue, too much flattery and currying favor with the queen. He refused to become involved in any court politics. Something happened to change his situation.

In the summer of 1861, a revolution broke out in Spain. The leaders were against royalty and the clergy. To save her life the queen escaped to Paris, taking Archbishop Claret with her. During his exile in France, Father Claret was able to attend the First Vatican Council in Rome. After he spoke on the infallibility of the pope, the council accepted the new doctrine.

Back in France, Archbishop Claret was pursued by revolutionaries from Spain. He had to move from one hiding place to another. Then the insurgents tried to bring him back by force. This was when he hid in the Cistercian monastery near Narboone. By then, the archbishop had become very sick and weak. He died there on October 24, 1879.

Over his tomb were carved these words: "I have loved justice and hated iniquity; therefore I die in exile." Several years later, the Claretian Order he had founded moved his remains to its monastery in Spain. Archbishop Claret was beatified by Pope Pius XI on February 25, 1934, and canonized on May 7, 1950, by Pope Pius XII. Today there are Claretian priests preaching missions all over the world. His feast day is October 23.

South America

St. Toribio de Mogrovejo
The Walking Saint of Peru
1538-1606

While serving as the archbishop of Peru, Toribio de Mogrovejo traveled forty thousand miles by mule and on foot. He made three such diocesan visits, dying far from home on the last. A man of astounding determination, this Spanish nobleman turned priest visited every parish in his vast diocese. It included all of Peru, Ecuador, Bolivia, Colombia, and Argentina. His travels put him in constant danger from weather, disease, wild animals, and Indians.

Toribio was born in Spain on November 16, 1538, in the province of Leon. His father was the powerful Duke of Mogrovejo, but Toribio, the second son, could never succeed to the title. As often happened in those days, he became a priest, but not right away.

Just when Toribio was about to enter the seminary, his father died. It became his duty to care for his mother, Ana de Robles, and his sister, until they were married or died.

Once his family was settled, Toribio changed direction. He began to study law at the University of Valladolid. Eventually he became a doctor of canon and civil law. Nevertheless, throughout those years of study, Toribio remained very devout, as he had been in his boyhood. He prayed the daily Office and gave generously to the poor.

Toribio was such an outstanding lawyer that the Spanish king, Philip II, appointed him head of the Inquisition in Granada. As a man of heart, he judged everyone fairly, whatever their station in life.

In 1575, the bishop of Lima, Peru, died. Even though Toribio was a layman, the king chose him to be the next archbishop.

During the two years before sailing to the New World, Toribio was ordained a deacon, then a priest. Two years later in Seville, the new priest was consecrated bishop, but the captain of his ship, crossing the wide ocean, failed to take his passengers to the correct port. Instead, he disembarked them at Payta, six hundred miles from Lima. Alone in a strange land, the new archbishop walked six hundred miles over mountains and through marshes to his diocese in Lima. His clothes looked so filthy and ragged, none could believe he was a prince of the Church.

Archbishop Mogrovejo began his work with great enthusiasm. His special interest was the care and conversion of the Peruvian Indians. Archbishop Toribio was shocked and very upset with the lifestyle of the Spaniards. Above all, they treated Blacks and Indians with terrible abuse and cruelty.

In spite of all this wickedness, Lima, Peru, produced five important saints while Toribio was archbishop: St. Martin de Porres, St. Francis Solano, St. John Casias, and St. Rose of Lima, whom he confirmed when she was eight. He himself was canonized in 1726.

Although he was of noble birth and a doctor of law, Archbishop Toribio never took advantage of his high position, living simply. He undertook severe penances, prayed, and fasted. When a deadly plague ravaged his flock, Archbishop Toribio walked in penitential processions, imploring God to save his city from sickness and death.

The saintly archbishop slept only four hours a night, dedicating every waking moment to his work. "Time is not our own," he often said. "We will have to give a strict account to God." He started the first seminary in South America and translated the catechism, possibly the first book printed in the New World. He called several councils of all eleven bishops in his archbishopric and built churches, convents, and orphanages.

He made three visitations of eighteen thousand miles each to all the villages and towns in his diocese. One time he was attacked by the Indians of Guanacuma, who aimed their poisonous arrows at him. During another journey, he visited two Indian tribes that were at war. When Archbishop Toribio entered one of the camps, he was struck by a volley of arrows.

At the age of sixty-eight, Archbishop Toribio made his third and final trip. Struck by a deadly fever, the archbishop struggled to continue on. He didn't want to disappoint those expecting to be confirmed, or priests looking for counsel. A hundred miles from Lima, he died at Sana on March 26, 1606.

The holy archbishop was beatified in 1679 and canonized in 1726. His feast day is April 27.

St. Louis Bertrand
Patron of Colombia
1526-1581

*S*t. Louis Bertrand was an amazing Dominican priest. He changed the lives of thousands and converted twenty-five thousand Indians during his seven years in South America, but sometimes he made enemies.

Father Bertrand criticized some noblemen in a sermon, and one became furious. The angry nobleman stopped the gentle priest and aimed his pistol at him. When Father Bertrand made the sign of the cross over the gun, it miraculously turned into a crucifix. The nobleman fell to his knees and begged forgiveness.

The story spread quickly, attracting crowds to Father Bertrand's sermons. When no church could hold all the people, he preached at the town square.

This remarkable priest was born in Valencia, Spain, on January 21, 1526. His father, Juan Bertrand, was a notary. He was related to St. Vincent Ferrer and, like the fifteenth–century saint, was very devout. Louis's mother, Juana, was often sick, and died very young.

In his teens Louis twice ran away, hoping to enter

Valencia's Dominican monastery, but his father objected. When nearly nineteen, he won his father's permission and entered the Dominican order.

Louis studied very hard, and was ordained a priest in 1547 at the age of twenty-three. Two years later he was appointed novice master, holding that position for six years.

Wanting to understand theology better, he left to study at the University of Salamanca. It was soon after his return that Father Bertrand became so famous for his sermons.

When a deadly plague broke out in Valencia, Father Bertrand nursed the sick and comforted the dying. He took no care for his own safety, but by his devotion demonstrated his love of neighbors.

Father Bertrand's holiness and wisdom spread throughout Spain. He became so well known that the great St. Teresa of Avila wrote to him for spiritual advice.

Then Father Beltran learned of the great need for missionaries in the New World. It was only sixty years after Christopher Columbus discovered America.

In 1562, Father Bertrand, with two other Dominican priests, set sail for Colombia, a country in northern South America. They landed in Cartagena, the major port on the Caribbean Sea. Father Bertrand learned the various Indian dialects, and during his seven years made twenty-five thousand converts. He traveled all over Colombia, from the coastal villages to the capital of Bogotá, the capital, high in the Andes Mountains.

He also preached and baptized many natives in Panama and Venezuela. When a dangerous Carib Indian gave Father Bertrand a poisonous drink, the priest might have died, but to the Indian's amazement, he vomited up the concoction and a fistful of snakes. The Indian instantly asked to be baptized.

Father Bertrand also sternly preached to the Spanish colonists about their cruel treatment of the Indians and African slaves. This turned many settlers against him, resulting in four attempts on his life. He survived, but began to suffer poor health from tropical diseases. He asked the Dominican superior to let him return to Spain.

Home again in Valencia, Father Bertrand was elected superior of the Dominican order and then master of novices. The holy man preached his last sermon in the Cathedral of Valencia. Shaking with fever, he was carried back to the monastery. After suffering for two years, he died on October 5, 1581. He was beatified on June 26, 1608, and Pope Clement V pronounced him a saint on April 12, 1671. He was declared patron of Colombia in 1690, and his feast day is October 10.

St. Martin de Porres
The Black Saint of Peru
1570-1639

*M*artin de Porres was born in Lima, Peru, on December 9, 1570. He was baptized in the Church of St. Sebastian. His father, Don Juan de Porres, was a Spanish knight. He came to the New World to become governor of Panama. There he fell in love with a black woman named Anna Velusquez. She was not a slave, but a free resident.

Don Juan took Anna with him when he moved to Lima. There she gave birth to Martin. Two years later they had another baby, Joan. Due to his high position, Don Juan never married Anna because she was black.

After living in Lima for eight years, Don Juan deserted Anna and her children. Anna had to go to work to support them. The black mother and her mulatto son, Martin, were reduced to poverty. Sometimes Don Juan sent money for his son's education, so Martin had a few years of schooling.

But young Martin was devoted to his Church. He

served at Mass every morning before going to school or work. Anna often found him on his knees, praying behind the privacy of a curtain. Martin loved all of God's creatures, even frogs and mice. He often brought home injured birds and animals, lovingly nursing them back to health.

At the age of twelve, Martin was apprenticed to a barber. In those days barbers were also surgeons. They knew a lot about herbs and medications. This knowledge came in handy for the kindly boy. Although he had very little money, Martin gave part of his earnings to his mother. The rest he gave away to the poor.

Martin was only fifteen when he decided to offer his life to God. He applied at the Dominican monastery, asking to live there as a servant. He scrubbed the floors, prepared the meals, and nursed any brothers who were sick. He also tilled a plot of ground. There he grew fruits and vegetables and gave them to the poor.

The brothers explained to Martin that it was not right for him to work as their servant, but that he should become a brother like him. Martin was so humble that he didn't feel worthy to become a Religious, but he did join the Third Order Dominicans. After that, he was called

"Brother Martin" and wore the order's white habit.

The year Martin turned twenty-four, the superior allowed the saintly youth to take the vows of poverty, chastity, and obedience. At last he was a friar like the others.

Brother Martin was a perfect friar. He became known for his goodness and the love he showed to everyone. When his monastery fell into debt, Brother Martin begged the superior to sell him as a slave to pay the money they owed, but the superior refused. Brother Martin knew all about slaves and slavery. When African slaves were brought to Peru, Brother Martin went down to the docks, where he cared for the sick and injured. They were black, just as he was.

Brother Martin became known for his miracles. He healed both people and animals. One day Martin passed a donkey with a broken leg. He felt sorry for the poor donkey and commanded it, "Creature of God, be cured." Instantly, the donkey stood up and trotted away.

There were many orphans begging on the streets of Lima, and Brother Martin raised money from the rich to build them an orphanage. He himself was sweet and innocent like a child, and everyone loved him. No one cared that he was black.

Every race and class loved the kindly friar. Soon everyone in Lima spoke about his many miracles. Trees he planted bore fruit all year. He was seen to float above the ground. Some even saw him in two places at once. Brother Martin did many penances to grow in love of God. He wore an itchy hair shirt, and a chain around his waist. In Lent he took only bread and water.

Every summer people in Lima came down with a deadly fever. One year the fever was extra bad. Brother Martin, who always cared for others, fell sick himself. As the weeks passed he became worse. He told the sad brothers standing around his bed, "I am going to die. I will pray for all of you in heaven." Then he asked each of them for forgiveness.

Brother Martin died that morning on November 3, 1639. He was almost seventy. When the people of Lima learned of his death, crowds came to the chapel to view his body, especially slaves and the poor. The rich and important also attended his funeral. Brother Martin was buried the next day. Miracles began to happen for everyone who prayed for his help. His skull is preserved in a crystal bowl above the altar of the monastery.

He was declared blessed in Rome by Pope Gregory XVI on August 8, 1837. He was canonized on May 6, 1962, by Pope John XXIII. St. Martin de Porres is patron of all who work to improve race relations. His feast day is celebrated on November 3 in Latin America, and on November 5 throughout the rest of the world.

St. Peter Claver
Slave to the Slaves, Colombia
1581-1654

*P*eter Claver was born near Barcelona, Spain, on February 6, 1581. His father was a well-to-do farmer. When Peter told him about his wish to become a priest, his father approved. His mother was very devout and proud of her son's decision.

Peter became a Jesuit, entering the order's novitiate in 1601. He studied for the priesthood at the University of Barcelona, and on Mallorca Island. While on that beautiful island he met Father Alfonso de Sandoval, who told Peter of the terrible plight of African slaves. Peter wanted to help them, as Father Sandoval had already done. He set sail for South America in 1610 to begin his work of mercy.

During the sixteenth and seventeenth centuries, several million West Africans were captured and shipped to the New World, mostly to work in the West Indies. They were chained and packed in the stinking holds of ships. At least half of the slaves died during the two-

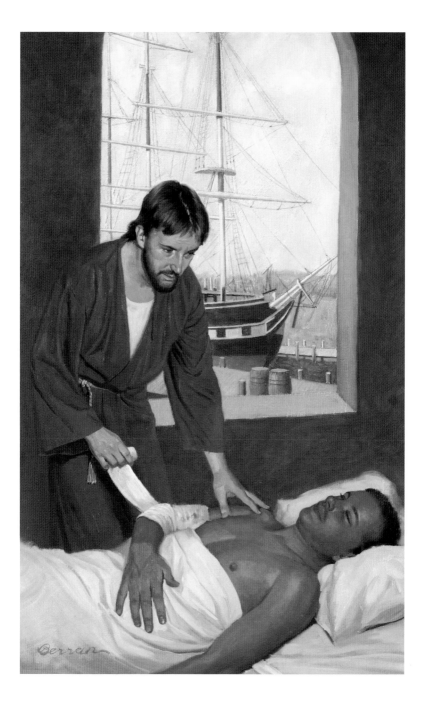

month voyage from Africa.

Cartagena, Colombia, was a major port on the Caribbean Sea. Slave traders generally brought their valuable cargo to Cartagena. Each time a slave ship arrived, Peter went aboard the ship to give them food and medicines. Once the slaves disembarked, they were penned in the holding yards until buyers purchased them.

In 1615, Peter was ordained at Bogotá, the capital of Colombia. Now, as a priest, Father Claver visited the slaves, caring for the sickest, whom no one else would touch. He brought interpreters who spoke African tribal languages, who translated his talks and sermons. He also showed pictures of Bible scenes as a teaching aid. In this way, Father Claver converted and baptized as many as a thousand slaves a year.

During his forty years in Cartagena, Father Claver baptized three hundred thousand African slaves.

Father Claver often preached in Cartagena's main plaza, urging slave owners to treat their slaves in a Christian manner. Many owners were brutal and considered slaves to be animals. Father Claver also visited the great plantations outside the city, where he chose to sleep in the slave quarters. He begged the cruel owners to treat their slaves better. Father Claver insisted, "We must speak to them in service to their needs, before speaking with our lips."

Whenever praised for the saintly work he was doing among God's most miserable creatures, Father Claver replied, "If being a saint consists in having no taste buds and owning a strong stomach, then I am a saint."

In 1650, Cartagena was stricken with a deadly plague. Father Claver continued his work among the slaves, and became one of the first victims of the deadly disease. He lay in his cell, growing weaker by the month. His black caretaker, fearing the plague, abandoned Father Claver. He died alone on September 8, 1654.

Peter Claver was beatified by Pope Pius IX in 1850, and was canonized on January 15, 1888, by Pope Leo XIII. Eight years later, that same pontiff named St. Peter Claver patron of all missionary activities to blacks.

The incorrupt body of St. Peter Claver rests in a glass case beneath the altar of Cartagena's ancient cathedral. His feast day is September 9.

St. Isabel de Santa Maria de Flores
St. Rose of Lima, Peru
1586-1617

*S*t. Rose of Lima was born Isabel de Santa Maria de Flores in Lima, Peru, in 1586. She was a beautiful child, and her parents expected her to marry a wealthy and important man. But even then the future saint took no interest in worldly matters. She dedicated her entire life to God.

As a little girl, Isabel spent much of her time praying in a little arbor her brother made for her in their garden.

At her confirmation Isabel took the name Rose, by which she was known ever after. Rose chose as her spiritual mentor the great Italian mystic St. Catherine of Siena. Soon Rose began practicing the austerity and severe penances of her medieval model. The young girl fasted to extremes and spent only a few hours in sleep. Her parents began to worry about their daughter's health.

Rose never entered a convent, but remained at home with her parents. However she wore the habit of the

Third Order Dominicans. Rose's parents built her a hermitage in their garden, where she remained for most of her short life. Word of the saintly young woman spread throughout Lima. Many people came to her hermitage asking for her prayers. Rose also had a great compassion for the poor and hungry of her city. She handed out bread to the needy at the garden gate. To earn money for her charities, Rose did beautiful embroidery, which she sold to the wealthy ladies of Lima.

As time passed, rumors spread about Rose's mystical experiences. She received visions and heard voices, and became regarded as a special saint of God. Because of Rose's unusual experiences, a commission of priests and doctors was sent to examine her. Many thought she had lost her mind, but Rose answered all their questions in a normal and intelligent manner. After conferring with one another, the scholarly gentlemen decided her visions came from God. Her fame spread.

Twice Rose saved her city from disaster. One time pirates landed on the coast of Peru. They marched inland to sack Lima of all its gold and silver treasures, but Rose's prayers drove them off. Her prayers also caused the defeat of Indians, who stormed the city's gates.

Rose's prayers even held power over nature. A terrible earthquake struck Peru, but Lima was spared. Everyone honored their wonderful Rose. Still a young woman, Rose fell desperately ill, most likely from her excessive penances. Don Gonsalo and his wife took Rose into their home, nursing her through the last three years of her life. She died there on August 24, 1617.

Her relics lie under the altar of Lima's Dominican church. In 1669, Rose was beatified and a great basilica was erected to honor her. She was canonized by Pope Clement X in 1671, the first native-born saint of the New World. St. Rose of Lima is patroness of all Latin America and the Philippines.

Her feast day is August 23.

St. Mariana de Paredes
The Lily of Quito, Ecuador
1618-1645

Quito, the capital of Ecuador, was built on the site of an ancient Incan city. It sits high in the Andes Mountains, far from the Pacific coast. Quito was settled by the Spanish in 1534. Not much later, a nobleman of Toledo left Spain and sailed to Peru, hoping to collect a debt.

Jeronimo de Paredes never returned to Spain. He married a wealthy girl of Quito named Mariana. The couple moved into her family's big stone house and started a large family of their own.

Mariana, the youngest of their eight children, was born on October 31, 1618, and baptized on November 22. Mariana was only four when her father, Jeronimo, died. Her mother passed away soon after. The orphaned little girl was raised by her oldest sister, Jeronima, who had married Captain Cosmo de Caso. Mariana's chief playmates were her sister's three little girls.

Learning about the martyrs of Japan who had just been canonized, the four children decided to run away and become martyrs, too. The little girls were found several miles outside the city, and were scolded severely. That same year, Mariana made her First Communion. She was deeply moved by the experience. Her behavior improved, and she took a vow to remain a virgin her entire life.

When Mariana reached seventeen, Captain de Caso offered her a dowry so she could enter the Poor Clares convent, but the serious teenager preferred to live at home as a Religious. Mariana moved into a bare, second-story room of her sister's house. There she lived as a nun.

Mariana began to live an austere life, praying and fasting. Her only food was the sacramental host. She wore a long, black dress and veil, and only left the house to attend Mass. She changed her name to Mariana of Jesus.

Mariana lived a simple life. After a night of three hours of sleep on a hard bed, Mariana rose at 4 a.m. She attended two Masses, recited the Little Office and the Rosary. At midday, Mariana gave out loaves of bread to the poor.

Mariana also took care of many sick people, and even raised a patient from the dead. In addition, the young woman did beautiful lace and embroidery, giving the proceeds to the needy. When Mariana made the sign of the cross on patients' foreheads, countless were healed instantly of their illness.

Near Quito stood a live volcano. One day the volcano began shooting red–hot lava on the city. Two thousand innocent victims were killed. Everyone in Quito expected to die.

That Sunday, Mariana stood up at Mass and offered her life if God would cause the volcano to stop. Quito also suffered deadly epidemics along with terrible earthquakes. They each ended whenever Mariana offered her life.

Finally, Mariana herself came down with a mysterious illness. A high fever wracked her body. She shook all over and suffered terrible pain, but her prayers caused the earthquakes to stop. A doctor came every day to bleed the suffering girl. Her Indian maid poured out Mariana's blood in the garden. In each place the blood fell, lilies sprang up from the ground. That was how she got the name Lily of Quito.

Mariana never recovered from that illness. After receiving the Last Rites, the holy woman died on May 26,

1645. She was buried in the habit of a member of the Third Order Franciscans. Her body rests under the altar of the church of Our Lady of Love in Quito.

Over two centuries passed before Mariana was beatified on November 10, 1853. Still another century later, in July 1950, she was canonized by Pope Pius XII. St. Mariana of Jesus, the Lily of Quito, is the patroness of Ecuador. Her saint's day is celebrated on June 2. She is also Ecuador's national heroine.

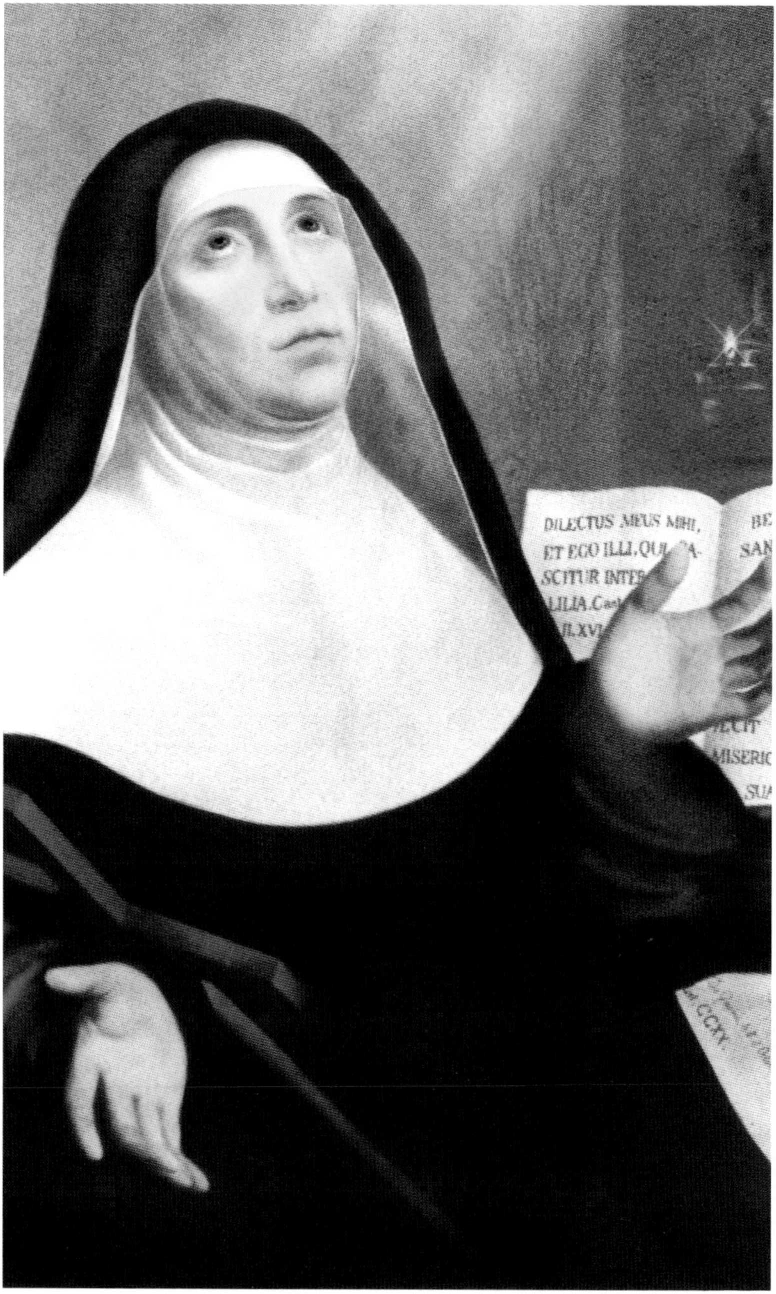
DILECTUS MEUS MIHI,
ET EGO ILLI,

Canada

Blessed Marie Guyard Martin
Marie of the Incarnation
1599-1672

*T*he future saint was born on October 28, 1599, a century after Christopher Columbus discovered America. She was from Tours, France. Her mother came from an important family, her father, Claude Guyard, was a baker.

From early childhood Marie was deeply devout, hoping someday to become a nun, but her parents had higher ambitions for her. When their daughter turned seventeen, they married her off to Claude Martin, a silk manufacturer. Two years later, Martin died, leaving Marie a widow with a little boy, named Claude. Now she was free to become a nun, except she had a son to raise. When he turned twelve, she sent him to the Benedictine monastery, and she joined the newly established Ursuline order. Her only child studied for the priesthood, and eventually became a Benedictine monk.

Only two years, after entering the convent at Tours, Marie, now Sister Marie of the Incarnation, was named novice mistress. A few years later the zealous sister felt called to the New World to save souls. France had established a colony in Canada. Its first city was Quebec.

In 1639, Sister Marie, with three other Ursulines, sailed from Dieppe for New France (Canada). The voyage to America took three months. They arrived in Quebec on July 4. At first they lived in a tiny wooden house. It provided little shelter from Canada's icy winters, but in 1641 the foundation was laid for a large stone building. It became the Ursuline convent. Marie was appointed superior.

The French settlers were thrilled to have the Ursulines in their town. The sisters brought stability and education to the rough pioneer colony.

Soon after her arrival, Mother Marie began studying various tribal languages. After all, she had traveled thousands of miles to bring Christianity to the Indians. Some received her teaching with joy, but the warlike Iroquois caused her great troubles. Several times they attacked Quebec; then, a fire destroyed the new convent. That winter, the sisters suffered terribly from the cold.

Mother Marie accepted every tribulation, glad to suffer for Christ. Nothing deterred her zeal. By 1651, the rebuilt convent was complete. The Ursuline academy became the finest school for young ladies in French Canada. Besides teaching there, and converting the Indians, Mother Marie kept a diary. It gives a detailed history of her life in New France, covering the years 1639 to 1671. She also wrote a new catechism for use of her students, called an *Explication*.

Mother Marie compiled dictionaries for the Algonquin and Iroquois, and continued to teach the Indians until her death on April 30, 1671. The Ursuline convent still remains in Quebec.

Mother Marie of the Incarnation (Marie Guyard Martin) was beatified in 1980 by Pope John Paul II.

St. Isaac Jogues and Companions
First North American Martyrs
1607-1646

*I*n 1603, Samuel de Champlain sailed up the St. Lawrence River and claimed the Canadian wilderness for France. He also founded Quebec. The area was populated by various Indian tribes. Some of them were friendly, others were not, and for years the only white men were a few hunters and trappers.

Across the Atlantic in France, several dedicated priests offered to go to New France (Canada). They wanted to convert the Indians and educate them. The best known of these was the martyred Jesuit, Father Isaac Jogues.

Isaac was born on January 10, 1607, in Orleans, France. His father was an important and wealthy official, who died soon after Isaac was born. The boy was raised by his mother, who taught him to love God and His Church. It was no surprise when Isaac asked to join the Society of Jesus.

He was accepted and went to Rouen for his novitiate.

College at La Fleche. Isaac was ordained a priest on February 9, 1636. The next day he said his first Mass.

Only three months later, at the age of twenty-nine, he sailed from Dieppe on a three-month voyage to Canada. In Quebec he met Father Anthony Daniel, another Jesuit. Father Daniel had already opened a school for Indian boys near Lake Huron. He asked Father Jogues to join him and aid in bringing the Indians to Christianity.

Five other Jesuits were already working among the Hurons, the most peaceful of the Indian tribes. Father Joques's main project was to learn the Huron language so he could teach them and preach. Father Jean de Brebeuf, who arrived in Quebec in 1625, was his instructor.

However, their work among the Hurons was difficult. The tribe's medicine men were against the Christian religion. After the priests baptized a thousand Indians, most of them children, the medicine men condemned the Jesuits to death. At a final ceremony before their execution, Father Brebeuf, the Jesuit superior, gave such a convincing talk about life after death, that the Indians spared his life and that of the other priests as well.

After their release, Father Jogues and Father Brebeuf were sent to open a new mission in Ontario. Their first year, the priests baptized one hundred twelve Indians. Two years later, they were sent to an area between Lake Huron and Lake Ontario. They made the trip on snowshoes, but on the way their Indian guides deserted them.

After a month of travel with little rest or food, they reached their destination. There they were threatened by the chiefs, who made them leave Ontario. At every village, the Jesuits were turned away.

Father Jogues decided they should return to Quebec for more supplies. He and several friendly Indians set out by canoe on the St. Lawrence River. After thirty-five days of paddling and portaging, the group reached Montreal where after a few days of rest, they left for Quebec.

At Quebec, Rene Goupil joined Father Jogues for the next trip to the Hurons. Rene was not a priest, but a lay associate who had studied surgery.

The party of forty left Quebec on August 1, 1642. On the second day out, the four Frenchmen and thirty-six Hurons were attacked by fierce Iroquois. Three Hurons were killed; the rest escaped into the woods.

The Frenchmen were taken prisoner and treated cruelly on the long march to the Iroquois' village. Later ,

Father Jogues reported the events to his Jesuit superior. He wrote, "The Indians struck me with sticks and their fists. Then they later tore out my fingernails and started biting my forefingers, which caused incredible pain. Rene Goupil suffered the same torments. What I endured is known to One for whose love and cause is a glorious thing to suffer for." One bit off a finger on his left hand. With his hands so mutilated, Father Jogues could no longer celebrate Mass.

Forced through several villages, the Frenchmen were beaten and burned with red-hot coals. On September 29, 1642, an Indian killed Rene Goupil with a tomahawk blow to the head. Father Jogues reported, "He was a man of unusual simplicity and innocence. He was killed for making the sign of the cross on the foreheads of Indian children."

Later the Indians took Father Jogues with them on an expedition to Fort Orange (now Albany, the capital of New York). It lay in the Dutch area of New York. By command of the Dutch governor, Father Jogues was freed for three hundred pieces of gold as ransom. He was then smuggled aboard a ship anchored in the Hudson River, which took him to New Amsterdam, where he sailed home to France. There the brave priest was honored as a living martyr. Even though his hands were deformed with fingers missing, Pope Urban VIII granted him a dispensation to say Mass.

In spite of all his sufferings in Canada, Father Jogues asked his superior to send him back. This time John de Lalande, a lay associate, went with him. They left France in 1644, going first to Montreal. Father Jogues sent a message from there to the Iroquois chiefs, asking that they have a peace powwow. Father Jogues and John de Lalande spent a week having a council with the Iroquois chiefs. Then they left for Quebec. As Father Jogues planned to go back to the Indian's village, he left a box of religious articles behind. These would be the cause of his death.

On Father Jogues's third visit to the Iroquois, he brought John along and they were attacked on the way. The Indians were desperate because their crops had failed and a fever had sickened their people. Being superstitious, they blamed everything on the box Father Jogues had left in their village.

A council of chiefs decided the Frenchmen's fate. On October 18, 1646, Father Jogues was beheaded, and the next day John de Lalande and his Huron guide were also killed. This tragedy took place near Auriesville, forty miles from Albany. A shrine there honors the French martyrs.

In 1649, Father Jean de Brebeuf and Father Gabriel Lalemont were cruelly tortured and finally killed by the Iroquois. Fathers Charles Garnier, Anthony Daniel, and Father Noel Chabanel were murdered by a Huron.

On June 23, 1925, the eight Jesuit martyrs were beatified by Pope Pious XI. Five years later he canonized them on June 25, 1930. Their feast day is held in Canada and the United States on October 19.

St. Marguerite Bourgeoys
Teacher of Girls
1620-1700

*T*he young Frenchwoman gazed up at the tall sailing ship. It was ready to embark from the seaport of Nantes for Quebec, Canada. The voyage across the Atlantic was thousands of miles. She wondered if the decrepit *Saint Nicholas* could make it as she bravely walked up the gangplank.

The young woman was right to be concerned. Only a few days after setting sail, the ancient vessel began to sink. The captain turned back to port, and the crew and passengers transferred to another ship. It made the two-month voyage successfully and arrived in Quebec on September 22, 1652. The young woman spent two weeks sailing up the St. Lawrence River before arriving in Montreal, her destination.

The young woman was the future saint, Marguerite Bourgeoys. At thirty-two, she had traveled to Canada to teach the handful of children in the recently founded city of Montreal.

Marguerite was born on April 17, 1620, in Noyes,

France. When Marguerite was seventeen, her mother died in childbirth. Marguerite cared for her motherless sister.

When Marguerite turned twenty, she felt a strong call to the Religious life. It began one day during a procession honoring the Virgin Mary. Marguerite thought the statue called her to give up everything. As a result, the young woman dedicated her life to God.

Soon Marguerite applied to two convents; both turned her down. Then, she and two friends started a community of their own, and they opened a school dedicated to teaching poor children. When the school had to close, Marguerite was asked to go to Montreal in New France (Canada). There she taught the seven children in the small colony of Montreal.

The school was in a little fieldstone building with dirt floors that had first been used as a stable. Marguerite also lived there, caring for three little Indian girls who attended her school.

In 1659, Marguerite, now known as Sister Bourgeoys, returned to France. She hoped to find other young women to help her. Three offered to go and teach in Canada's second colony. They arrived back in Montreal in October 1660.

Marguerite and the new teachers began to live like nuns. They wore long black dresses and black bonnets tied under the chin, with white veils.

In 1669, the bishop of Quebec visited Montreal and recognized Sister Bourgeoys' ladies as a religious community. They named it the Congregation of Notre Dame of Montreal. The following year, Sister Bourgeoys made another trip to France, where she recruited nine more sisters for her order.

By 1679, the growing congregation was established in five different places. Several were in Indian villages to help Iroquois children.

Now called Mother Marguerite, the founder helped raise funds to build the first stone church in Montreal.

At the age of sixty, Mother Marguerite made a third voyage home to France, seeking approval for her order. While she was gone, the motherhouse in Montreal burned to the ground. Two sisters died in the fire. To replace their lost convent, Mother Marguerite was given the two stone towers that had served as a fort on the top of Mount Royal. One tower was used as a school for Indian girls; the other served as a convent for the Sisters.

On June 24, 1679, Mother Marguerite's order finally received approval from the bishop. Their rule was accepted and the sisters took vows of poverty, chastity, and obedience. They took a fourth vow to commit their lives to working with young girls.

Mother Marguerite died on January 17, 1700, after almost a century of dedication to God. Her order continued to grow. By 1956, there were four thousand Notre Dame sisters in seven countries. Mother Marguerite Bourgeoys was beatified by Pope Pius XII on November 12, 1950. She was canonized by Pope John Paul II on October 31, 1982. Her feast day is January 12.

St. Marguerite d'Youville
Founder of the Grey Nuns
1701-1771

*U*nlike most Canadian saints, Marguerite Dufrost de Lajemmerais was born on October 15, 1701, far from France in Varennes, near Montreal. Marguerite's father died when she was small. Her mother and the six children moved to a farm where they could raise their own food, but the little town provided no chance for an education. At the age of eleven, Marguerite was sent to boarding school in Quebec under the care of the Ursulines. Besides the usual subjects, Marguerite learned to sew and crochet, which later helped her earn a living.

When Marguerite was almost grown up, her mother realized the best chance for her daughter making a good marriage was in Montreal. There the pretty young lady attended teas and dances, and met François d'Youville, a proud, spoiled young man. He was handsome and wealthy and seemed a good match. Marguerite and Francois were married on August 13, 1722. They had three children, but only two sons lived to maturity. Both sons became priests.

The children were still young when Francois got into serious financial trouble. He had been selling liquor to the Indians, and earned a terrible reputation as a drunkard. He died in 1730, leaving his wife and children nothing but debts.

The young widow never lost hope. She moved into the elder d'Youville's home and, using skills she learned at school, opened a dressmaking shop. It was so successful she was able to pay off all her husband's debts. His misfortunes made her turn to Christ for help, which led her to join the Confraternity of the Holy Family. This, as well as a confessor who held the same beliefs, led Marguerite to help the poor, the sick, and homeless. Every day she prayed, "Lord, show me the path you wish me to follow."

Marguerite did not like living with her cruel mother-in-law, Madame d'Youville. God answered her prayers. Marguerite had earned enough money from her sewing to buy a house. There she took in the poor, the sick, and homeless. Eventually, the work became more than she could handle alone.

Three ladies came to join her. On November 21, 1737, the new order was formed, called the Sisters of Charity, and because they adopted a grey habit, they became know as the "Grey Nuns."

In 1745, the sisters made their formal vows. Other women asked to join the order and the work expanded. The Grey Nuns took over the running of Montreal's General Hospital with Mother Marguerite as administrator. The hospital was old and run-down. Mother Marguerite raised money to get it out of debt, then repaired and enlarged it. In 1755, Bishop Henry Mary Du Breil de Pointbriand of Montreal appointed Mother Marguerite the superior of the Grey Nuns. Her order continued to grow.

Clothing that she made for trappers and soldiers was a main source of revenue for her order and the hospital. In 1766, Montreal's General Hospital burned to the ground. Putting all her trust in God, she raised enough funds to build a new hospital.

During the French and Indian War, Mother Marguerite ransomed an English prisoner from the Indians. The savages had planned to torture him until someone paid the ransom.

Mother Marguerite always accepted hardships and disappointments as from the hand of God, but looked for and found solutions, and worked toward them. She also proved that a married woman and mother could achieve sanctity.

During the last fifteen years of her life, Mother Marguerite took over the care of Quebec's hospitals. She started schools and orphanages, and her foundling home was the first in North America.

Mother Marguerite died in Montreal on December 23, 1771, at the age of seventy. Over the next two and a half centuries, her order opened charitable and missionary works on three continents. The Grey Nuns are particularly known for their work with the Eskimos in Alaska.

This saintly mother was beatified on May 3, 1959, by Pope John XXIII, and canonized by Pope John Paul II in 1990.

Her feast day is April 11.

Blessed Alfred Bessette
Brother Andre of St. Joseph's Oratory
1845-1937

*T*he young Holy Cross brother had a dream. In it he built a giant shrine to St. Joseph at the top of Mount Royale. Many years later, Brother Andre's dream came true!

Brother Andre was born Alfred Bessette on August 9, 1845, in St. Gregoire, Canada. Not expected to live, he was baptized the same day. The frail boy was the sixth of his parents' ten children.

The year Alfred was nine, his father was killed in a lumbering accident. He left no money for his children, who were sent to live with relatives. Alfred's aunt and uncle took him in. When the boy was twelve, he made his First Communion, which greatly impressed him.

Alfred's aunt and uncle were too poor to pay for his education. At thirteen he had to go out and earn a living. Unable to read or write, and sick more often than well, Alfred went from one lowly job to the next. He prayed constantly and attended Mass every day, but most of what he knew about Jesus and the Catholic Church he learned from sermons. He remembered passages he had heard and quoted them often.

The year Alfred turned twenty-five, he applied to join the Congregation of the Holy Cross. Because he couldn't write, Alfred asked his parish priest to compose the application. Alfred was accepted and entered the novitiate in 1870. He was given the name Brother Andre.

As the new brother was uneducated, he was assigned humble tasks, such as scrubbing floors and washing dishes, and was later sent to the orders' school for boys. There he worked as a porter, answering the door, distributing the mail, and welcoming visitors. This was his job for the next forty years.

Each day with his duties, Brother Andre would visit the sick in their homes or the hospital. Many were healed by his prayers. They came by his little office for counsel and were given hope. Soon the news of the humble brother's miracles spread around Montreal. Brother Andre always gave full credit to St. Joseph. He would insist, "I am only a man like you."

Owning nothing and uneducated, Brother Andre conceived the idea of building a chapel to St. Joseph, his

patron saint. He went to the archbishop and asked for funds to construct a place of worship on Mount Royale, the highest point in Montreal. The bishop said, "Go ahead and build it. Use whatever funds you can raise."

First, Brother Andre collected and saved nickels and dimes. He placed a basket for donations at the top of Mount Royale, and eventually Brother Andre had enough money to build a small, wooden chapel. As people began visiting it, they gave more. Brother Andre kept adding to the structure. Finally, a giant basilica rose at the crest of the five-hundred-foot hill. It could be seen from everywhere in Montreal, and took fifty years to complete.

Brother Andre lived in a tiny room next to the basilica. So many people came seeking his help that the little brother could barely find time to sleep. Eventually crutches, canes, casts, and even replicas of hearts and kidneys decorated the walls of what became known as St. Joseph's Oratory. They were left there by pilgrims who had been healed. Brother Andre became known as "The Saint of Mount Royale."

The little brother who had been sickly all his life lived to be ninety-one years old.

After his death on January 6, 1937, a million people braved the winter cold to climb the steep steps to the basilica. They stood in line to view the simple wooden casket of the beloved brother. Many wept at Montreal's great loss.

Yet it wasn't a loss, but a blessing. People still come from near and far to be healed at St. Joseph's Oratory. Brother Andre's tiny cell remains exactly as it looked those many years he lived in it. What had once been only a dream became Brother Andre's great accomplishment. He never stopped working for God and St. Joseph. Brother Andre was beatified on May 23, 1982. His saint's day is January 6.

United States

Blessed Kateri Tekakwitha
First Blessed Native American
1656-1680

Kateri Tekakwitha was born in 1656 at an Indian village near Auriesville, New York. On the Mohawk River, it is close to Albany, now the capital of New York. Her father was a Mohawk chief, her mother a Christian of the Algonquin tribe.

Kateri was only four when a smallpox epidemic swept through her village. Both of Kateri's parents died of the disease, and Kateri's face was covered with pockmarks, her eyes nearly blinded. Her aunts and an uncle took over her care.

In 1668, Jesuit priests came to her village. They taught the Indians about Jesus and the sacraments of the Catholic Church. Kateri was baptized a Catholic on Easter Sunday, April 5, 1676.

Most of her village rejected the new religion. The other Indians made fun of her and treated her cruelly.

Some pulled her long braids, others threw stones. It became dangerous for her to remain there. One day, two Christian braves hid Kateri in a canoe, and they paddled and walked two hundred miles to Canada. They finally arrived at the Christian village of St. Francis Xavier. Near Montreal, it was the same village Kateri's mother had come from. The trip took two months.

Jesuit priests had built a chapel there. Every morning, Kateri rose at 4 a.m. and stood by the chapel door until it was opened. She attended the early Mass every day, sometimes staying for two more Masses. Kateri took a vow not to marry, giving all her love to Jesus.

Kateri spent her days in acts of kindness and penance. She fetched water for the elderly, cooked for them and fed them, told the children stories about Jesus, and nursed anyone who fell sick. All the Christian Indians loved Kateri and called her "their little saint."

In 1679, Kateri fell ill. She was too weak to get out of bed. She couldn't eat. Her spiritual director, a Jesuit priest named Father Pierre Cholonec, brought Kateri communion and prayed with her for recovery, but there was no hope.

In 1680, only twenty-four-years old, the holy Indian

maiden died. The story of her goodness and sanctity spread across Canada and down into New York State. People of all races prayed to Kateri for favors, such as recovery from sickness, good crops, and safety in travel. Many of them were granted.

Kateri was baptized at Caughnawaga, which is on the grounds of the shrine in Fonda, New York. The National Shrine of Blessed Kateri Tekawitha is in Fonda, New York, and the Shrine of the North American Martyrs is in Auriesville, New York. Thousands visit them to pray to the holy Indian maiden, who became known as the "Lily of the Mohawks."

In 1943, Kateri was declared venerable, and on June 22, 1980, she was beatified by Pope John Paul II. Because her entire life was spent close to nature, she is considered the patron of ecology and the environment. There are five thousand members of the Blessed Kateri League, whose aim is to conserve nature and praise the Creator of all. Blessed Kateri's feast day is celebrated on July 14.

Blessed Junípero Serra
Founder of California's Missions
1713-1784

*O*ne of the most popular attractions in California is the string of Spanish missions along the Pacific coast. They were built by the Franciscan friar Junípero Serra in the eighteenth century.

Born Miguel Joseph Serra on November 21, 1713, in Petra on the island of Mallorca off the coast of Spain, he was later given the name Junípero, which means "Jester of God."

From his earliest years, Junipero dreamed of becoming a priest. On graduating from Palma University, he entered the Franciscan order at the age of seventeen. He was ordained in 1738. After taking his final vows, Father Serra was sent to teach at the University of Llallian, but his great wish was to go to the New World and bring the Gospel to the Indians.

Lower California, today a part of Mexico, was discovered in 1533 and claimed for Spain by Juan Cabrillo in 1542. Not until 1745 did the Spanish

government take action to occupy Upper California. Soon after Father Serra, with two other friars, set sail from Cadiz on August 30, 1749, for Mexico. The voyage to Vera Cruz took ninety-nine days. While the others traveled by horse and mule to Mexico City, Father Serra walked the hundreds of miles to the capital. On the way, the future saint was bitten by a poisonous insect. His foot became infected and swollen, but he continued on. The injury caused him pain for the rest of his life.

Arriving in Mexico City, he was assigned to teach philosophy at San Fernando University. He was there for nine years, all the time thinking of the Indians he hoped to convert.

Finally his chance came. In 1769, King Charles III of Spain ordered all the Jesuit priests out of Northern California. Then, he sent Father Serra there as president of California's missions. Upon arriving, Father Serra immediately founded the first mission, San Diego de Alcala. He next sailed to Monterey, the capital at that time, and founded St. Charles Borromeo Mission on the Carmel River. When not traveling, he lived there as his home base.

He traveled thousands of miles, mostly on foot,

founding seven more missions. Twenty-one missions eventually stretched for eight hundred miles along the California coast. Perhaps the most famous mission is San Juan Capistrano, known for yearly visits by flocks of swallows.

All the missions were in Spanish style and built of adobe and mud. Father Serra set up the first cross at San Diego as well as a small chapel, which had daily Masses. The Franciscan priest tied small bells to trees to attract the Indians. He learned the languages of seven different tribes, writing a catechism in each.

At the missions, Father Serra taught the Indians to farm, tan, and make leather articles, weave cloth and baskets, and grow oranges. His Indians were described as well-housed, well-fed, peaceful, and devout.

Eventually, the Franciscans established twenty-one missions in California, spreading the Catholic faith everywhere. From 1749 to 1784, Father Serra traveled constantly, improving the missions and encouraging the many friars in their work among the Indians.

But at the end of 1784, after more than thirty years of devoted work and travel, Father Serra died of tuberculosis at seventy-one. At his request, Father Serra was buried in the Carmel mission, where his remains rest today.

Father Serra was an important figure in the development of California. The war between Mexico and the United States, from 1846 to 1847, put an end to Mexican rule. In 1848, Mexico ceded California to the United States, and on September 9, 1850, it was admitted to the Union as a "free" state.

Following the miraculous healing from fatal lupus of Sister Mary Boniface Dryda, Pope John Paul II beatified the beloved friar on September 25, 1988. The Holy Father called Blessed Junípero Serra "a shining example of Christian virtue and the missionary spirit." His saint's day is July 1.

Venerable Pierre Toussaint
The Hairdresser Saint
1766-1853

*P*ierre Toussaint was born in 1766 on the West Indian island of Haiti. His parents were slaves, owned by Jean Berard and his wife, Marie.

The Berards were French colonists who owned a large plantation, where the work was done by slaves brought from Africa. They grew sugar, cotton, and coffee. All the wealthy colonists were royalists and Catholic. Pierre was baptized at the beautiful church in Cap Haitien.

Like the other house slaves, he was expected to work. But unlike most slave owners, the Berards were kind to Pierre, teaching him to read and write, even how to play the violin.

One day, in 1793, all the slaves in Haiti revolted. Masters who couldn't escape were murdered, but Pierre's owners had already boarded a ship sailing to New York, taking Pierre and his sister, Rosalie, with them.

In order for Pierre to earn money, Jean Berard apprenticed the young man to a New York hairdresser.

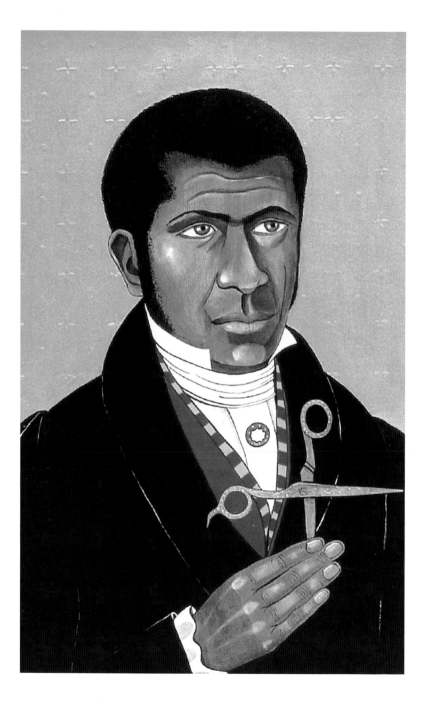

Pierre hoped to save money to buy his freedom, but Jean Berard died, leaving his widow penniless. With their plantation gone and the loss of all their investments, they were bankrupt.

In those days, all the wealthy ladies, such as Martha Washington, wore elaborate hairstyles, but they couldn't style their own hair. They sent for Pierre and paid him handsomely. He would walk to their homes and make them look beautiful. Though Pierre wanted to be free, he gave all of his wages to support Madam Berard and her children. She freed him on her deathbed.

Like the Berards, Pierre was a devout Catholic. Every day, Pierre attended the 6 a.m. Mass at old St. Peter's Church on Barclay Street. He never missed in forty years.

But that wasn't all. With Madam Berard gone, and her children married, Pierre was free to use his earnings as he pleased. He supported many Catholic charities, giving most of his wages to needy blacks and orphanages. He even was a principal donor to build New York's first St. Patrick's Cathedral, then downtown on Mulberry Street. Ironically, on Sunday, when he tried to attend Mass there, the ushers told him to leave because no blacks were allowed.

Pierre not only donated money to good causes, but brought faith and hope to the rich Protestant ladies he worked for. While fixing their coiffures, Pierre would quote passages from the Bible or St. Thomas Aquinas, and he would tell them stories from the sermons he had heard. Also, he encouraged his clients to pray.

He met a charming lady, Marie Rose Julliette, and she and Pierre were married in 1811 at St. Peter's.

He also raised his sister's daughter, Euphemie, after Rosalie died. Pierre was fearless. During a terrible yellow fever epidemic, Pierre went into the infected areas of New York City to nurse the sick. The disease was highly contagious and usually fatal.

He donated part of his wages to build the first black Catholic school in New York, and helped found an orphanage with St. Elizabeth Seton. When his customers were downcast and worried, Pierre advised his wealthy Protestant clients, "Jesus can give you nothing so precious as himself."

The Schuylers were one of New York's most prominent old Dutch families. Mary Ann Schuyler said of Pierre, "I have known Christians who were not gentlemen and gentlemen who were not Christian — but one man I know who is both, and he is black." She often referred to Pierre as "my saint."

How close to the truth she spoke. Pierre continued to work until he died on June 30, 1853. He was eighty-seven. All those years he attended daily Mass, contributing most of his earnings to charities. Pierre was buried at old St. Patrick's.

A century later, this very special man was still remembered. New York's Cardinal Terence Cooke opened the Cause for beatification of the humble hairdresser. Cardinal Cooke's successor, Cardinal John O'Connor, worked hard to forward Pierre's Cause in Rome. He was declared venerable by Pope John Paul II in 1996.

In 1992, the cardinal had Pierre's remains dug up and reburied in the crypt off Fifth Avenue's St. Patrick's Cathedral.

A little boy was born with a curvature of the spine in 1995. Once he would have been called a hunchback. Five-year-old Joey Peacock's parents prayed to Pierre for their son to be healed. He was.

If the miraculous healing of little Joey Peacock is accepted by the Holy See, Pierre Toussaint could become the first black saint in the United States.

St. Rose Philippine Duchesne
The Pioneer Nun
1769-1852

*R*ose Philippine Duchesne was born on August 29, 1769, in Grenoble, France. Her father was a lawyer, her mother a member of the prominent Perier family. Rose grew up in a castle and was instructed by a tutor, but at the age of twelve she was sent to a boarding school run by the Sisters of the Visitation. Their quiet, prayer-filled life impressed Rose, and she wanted to enter their order.

When she was eighteen, her parents chose a husband for he, but she secretly ran off and joined the Visitation convent. Then came the terror of the French Revolution. All convents and monasteries were closed, and many priests were executed. No longer allowed to wear her habit, Rose was forced to return home and live with her parents.

Rose formed a group called the Ladies of Mercy. They took care of the poor and sick and hid priests in danger. In 1801, the war ended and Rose's convent reopened. Three years later, Rose and four other Visitation sisters joined the recently new Order of the Sacred Heart. A year later the five sisters were professed.

Sister Rose had always dreamed of going to America as a missionary to the Indians. Her dream came true in 1817. Bishop Louis Dubourg, bishop of Louisiana, asked the mother superior of Sacred Heart to send some of her sisters to his diocese. The United States had just bought the Louisiana Territory from France. The French-speaking nuns would be a great help to him in the lands west of the Mississippi River.

Now called Mother Duchesne, she was accompanied by four other sisters. They set sail from Le Havre, spending eleven weeks at sea. After landing in New Orleans, they traveled another seven weeks up the Mississippi. They finally arrived in St. Louis, Missouri, where they were met by Bishop Dubourg.

To her great disappointment, the bishop sent Mother Duchesne to start a school for girls in St. Charles, instead of going to an Indian mission. The bishop warned the Sacred Heart sisters they would suffer many hardships. Mother Duchesne soon discovered he was right. There were shortages of food and clean water, and they were crowded into a cold log cabin. Their first little school served children with the rough manners of the Wild West. Still, Mother Duchesne continued praying for a chance to work with Indians.

Meanwhile, she opened schools in Grand Choteau, New Orleans, Florissant, and St. Michael. They were served by sixty-four sisters. Then, at last, Mother Duchesne's prayers were answered.

Father Pierre De Smet, a Jesuit missionary, asked Mother Duchesne and her sisters to work at his mission to the Potawatomi Indians. He presented them with five hundred dollars raised by Catholics in New Orleans, but by that time Mother Duchesne was seventy-two years old.

After another long, uncomfortable journey by boat and ox-cart, the sisters arrived at Sugar Creek Mission. They were greeted by five hundred Indian braves on horseback, whooping war cries and brandishing rifles. Mother Duchesne shook hands with each of the braves and hugged the squaws.

At a ceremonial dance that night, Father De Smet presented Mother Duchesne to the Indians, saying, "Here, my children, is the sister who has prayed for thirty-five years to come to you."

Mother Duchesne never learned the Potawatomi language, but she communicated with smiles. Nor could she work any longer. But she could still pray. The aged nun spent each day on her knees in the tiny chapel, praying for her Indians. They were so impressed with Mother Duchesne, they called her, "The woman who prays always."

The severe cold and lack of food took a toll on the elderly nun. The superior ordered her back to the motherhouse in St. Charles, Missouri. After ten years living quietly in the convent, Mother Duchesne died on November 18, 1852. She was eighty-three.

During her thirty-five years in the far west, Mother Duchesne had founded many schools and convents. In 1826, Pope Leo XII recognized the good work she had done. After her death, Mother Duchesne's work spread north and south, even to New York, where the famed Manhattanville College was started.

The devout Sacred Heart nun was beatified on May 12, 1940, and canonized by Pope John Paul II on July 3, 1988. Many come to pray at her tomb in St. Charles, Missouri. Her feast day is celebrated in America on November 18.

St. Elizabeth Ann Seton
First U.S.-Born Saint
1774-1821

*B*orn Elizabeth Ann Bayley in New York City in 1774, the future Catholic saint was baptized and raised in the Episcopal Church. Her father was a well-to-do doctor and socialite. Elizabeth's life would have been ideal if her mother had not died when she was little. Her father married again, and Elizabeth's stepmother was too busy with seven children of her own to bother with the lonely little girl.

When Elizabeth became a teenager she was sent to a finishing school. She was invited to balls and elegant parties, one time dancing with President George Washington.

In 1794, Elizabeth married William Seton, a wealthy young shipowner. They had three girls and two boys, but tragedy later struck the happy couple. Elizabeth's husband fell ill with tuberculosis; then, a terrible storm at sea sank all his ships.

Their doctor suggested Elizabeth take William to Italy

in hopes of curing his illness. They took their eldest daughter, Ana Maria, aged eight. William became sicker on the long voyage, and died a few weeks after they arrived in Leghorn, Italy, where all three were put in quarantine.

Alone in a foreign country, Elizabeth and her daughter were taken in by Italian friends of William Seton. They were devout Catholics, who took Elizabeth to their church. She was so impressed by the beauty of the Mass and the devotion of the worshipers that she decided to become a Catholic. She even adopted a black dress and cap, which eventually became the habit of her order.

On returning to New York, and after taking instruction in her new faith, Elizabeth and all five children were received into the Catholic faith.

Elizabeth's socialite relatives, however, were horrified that she had become a Catholic. They snubbed her and even refused to help the poor young widow, who had been left penniless.

To support her family, Elizabeth opened a small school in New York, but that didn't work out. Then she moved to Baltimore, where the archbishop invited her to open a Catholic school for girls. Soon after, Elizabeth decided to dedicate her life to Christ as a nun. She and four other women started a new order, the Sisters of Charity of St. Joseph. With ten thosand dollars donated by a young man, they bought land in Emmitsburg, Maryland, and opened a boarding school. Sister Seton took her three girls to the convent school with her. Then, another tragedy struck. Two of Elizabeth's daughters died young of tuberculosis, then one son, Richard, died at sea, but not all was so bleak. Later, her remaining daughter became a nun, and her eldest son, William, became an officer in the U. S. Navy, married, and had nine children.

Sister Seton started several schools and orphanages. She died in 1821 at the age of forty-seven. Her order has seven thousand sisters all over the world, and many schools and hospitals are named in her honor. She was canonized in 1974 by Pope John Paul II, and is the first U.S.-born saint. A huge shrine was built at Emmitsburg, where her remains are under the altar. Along with St. John Nuemann, St. Elizabeth Seton is considered one of the founders of the Catholic parochial-school system in America.

St. John Neumann
Second U.S.-Citizen Saint
1811-1860

*L*ittle John Nepomucene Neumann was always the shortest boy in his class. Even when he grew up and became a priest, he was only five feet two. Yet, he made up for his size with great energy for the Lord's work, and with the strength of Hercules in spreading the Gospel.

John Neumann was born on March 28, 1811, in Prachtitz, Bohemia, now in the Czech Republic. His parents, Philip and Agnes Neumann, had five other children. Theirs was a religious household, and from an early age John dreamed of becoming a priest. He was also talented at languages, and took a great interest in science and medicine.

John was an outstanding scholar. After graduating, he applied to enter the local seminary, but there were ninety applications for only twenty openings. Through his and his mother's ardent prayers, John learned he had been one of those accepted. He entered the seminary at Budweise on November 1, 1831, and later studied at Prague.

When it was time for his ordination, the bishop suddenly died and all ordinations had to be canceled, but all was not lost. John heard from Bishop John Dubois of New York that his diocese was in dire need of priests who spoke German. He asked John to come to America, but could afford to send him only his ocean passage.

So, on February 8, 1836, the ardent young man began his journey. Without funds for a stagecoach, John walked across Europe to LeHavre. There he boarded the *Europo* for the forty-day voyage to New York.

At that time, the Catholic Diocese of New York included the entire state, plus parts of New Jersey. Bishop Dubois assigned John to an area of nine hundred square miles, including the city of Buffalo. He ordained John in June 1836, before sending him off to northern New York, where there were already four hundred German families. Arriving in Williamsville, which had a small church (though it had no roof and only an earth floor), he built a small hut for himself.

The local Catholic families were overjoyed to have a German-speaking priest to hear their confessions and bring them the comforts of their Church. Not satisfied with just helping Catholics in adjoining towns, Father

Neumann set out to frontier towns carrying candles, hosts, and a chalice on his back.

Father Neumann was loved by everyone, even the Indians. One time on the way to say Mass, the little priest fell and was severely injured. He lay in pain on the ground for hours. A band of Indians found him. Using a blanket and poles for a litter, the Indians carried Father Neumann to his simple hut.

In time, Father Neumann realized he was lonely, and yearned for the fellowship of other priests. He asked to join the Redemptorists, and was accepted. He traveled by coach to Pittsburgh, where he entered the order. He became a U.S. citizen on February 10, 1848, in Baltimore, renouncing allegiance to the Austri an emperor.

Because he spoke eight languages, the little priest was able to help immigrants from many countries, who were alone and frightened in this new and strange land. His goodness and dedication didn't go unnoticed. Twice his order elected him superior. Then, in 1852, Pope Pious IX appointed Father Neumann the bishop of Philadelphia. It was one of the largest dioceses in America, with one hundred thirteen churches serving one hundred seventy thousand Catholics.

Bishop Neumann wanted every parish to have its own school. A founder of Catholic education in the United States, Bishop Neumann was the first to organize a diocesan Catholic school system. He increased the number of Catholic schools in his diocese from two to a hundred between 1852 and 1860. He also started hospitals, churches, orphanages, and a seminary, as well as Sts. Peter and Paul Cathedral.

No matter how bad the weather or how weak he felt, Bishop Neumann went wherever duty called him. One day, coughing and ill, Bishop Neumann left the Episcopal residence to go to the post office. There the bishop collapsed in the street. A priest and a doctor were sent for, but by the time they arrived the kindly bishop was gone. He was only forty-seven.

Once the Vatican was informed of the required miracle, Bishop Neumann was declared Blessed. He was canonized on June 19, 1977, by Pope Paul VI. His remains lie under the altar of the cathedral-basilica in Philadelphia, where he was so greatly loved. Bishop Neumann was the first male citizen of the United States to be canonized.

His feast day is January 5.

Blessed Joseph de Veuster
Father Damien: The Leper Priest
1840-1889

*T*he saint known as Father Damien was born Joseph de Veuster in Belgium in 1840. From the time Joseph was a boy, his only dream was to be a priest. On completing school, he entered the Congregation of the Sacred Heart and began his studies toward the priesthood. He was given the name Brother Damien.

His order was dedicated to foreign missionary work. One day Brother Damien read an article about the leprosy in Hawaii. He was horrified to see photos of the terrible ravages of leprosy. The lepers often lost fingers and toes because of the disease, or their faces would be scarred. Considered highly contagious and incurable, leprosy was the most feared of all diseases at the time. Lepers were always isolated from everyone, and forced to leave everything they knew and loved. Few people were brave enough to care for them.

But this was exactly what young Brother Damien resolved to do. He would give his life to the care of the lepers on far-off Molokai. Brother Damien arrived in Hawaii on March 18, 1864, where he was ordained a priest in the Cathedral of Our Lady of Peace in Honolulu.

That same year, King Kamehameha IV signed a law banishing all lepers in Hawaii to an undeveloped tract of land on the island of Molokai. There was no hospital, no doctors or nurses to care for them, and no food or shelter. The lepers were taken there on ships and thrown overboard, forced to swim to shore or drown.

Father Damien was the only person who offered to help the lepers. He arrived at Molokai on May 10, 1873. Only thirty-three, he was young and vigorous. He taught the lepers to build houses, even a chapel. Fearlessly, he washed and bandaged their wounds.

The lepers knew they were going to die, even the little children, because there was no cure. They lived lawless lives, drinking and fighting, but the young priest brought them order, hope, and love. In church, Father Damien addressed his unusual congregation as "My dear brothers." He even built coffins for those released from their suffering by death. At least he had brought them the comforts of the Catholic faith through the sacraments and his sermons.

Father Damien worked among the hundreds of lepers on Molokai for twelve years. Then, one morning in 1885, he woke up to discover no feeling in his fingers, and several white spots on his face. He had leprosy. The next Sunday, Father Damien stood up and told his congregation, "My fellow lepers, I am one of you now."

In spite of his pain and sickness, Father Damien continued to minister to the seven hundred lepers on the isolated island. Like them, he would never be allowed to leave Molokai. After four years of suffering, Father Damien died on April 15, 1889. He was forty-nine.

His story might have only been known to a small number of priests and missionaries in the far-off Hawaiian Islands. However, the famous novelist Robert Louis Stevenson visited Molokai and learned about the leper priest. He wrote an article praising Father Damien for his heroic life and sacrificial death, calling him "a saint and a hero." The story spread around the world, sending a message of Father Damien's Christian love. Many people were inspired to become missionaries; doctors searched to find a cure for the disfiguring disease.

That was not discovered until 1946. A drug called sulfone was tested on six patients with leprosy, producing amazing results. All lepers were given the drug. It was so successful that most leper colonies were closed and abandoned, including the one on Molokai.

Father Damien's imposing story is used in sermons and books to illustrate Christian love and dedication. Schools and hospitals are named in honor of the brave leper priest.

In 1898, Hawaii was annexed by the United States Congress, proceeding to a U. S. territory in 1900, becoming the fiftieth state in 1959. The once feared island of Molokai is now a luxury resort famed for its beautiful beaches and golf courses. Father Damien was declared venerable in 1977 by Pope Paul VI, and was beatified in Belgium by Pope John Paul II on June 4, 1995. Today, with Hawaii a state, he is honored as an American saint by many Hawaiians, though he is yet to be canonized by Rome.

St. Frances Xavier Cabrini
First U.S.-Citizen Saint
1850-1917

*F*rancesca Xavier Cabrini was born in 1850 in Saint Angelo, Italy. She was the thirteenth and last child of her middle-aged parents. Francesca was an obedient and devout child, mostly raised by an older sister. The future saint early dreamed of becoming a missionary to China.

Both her parents died when Francesca was seventeen. Applying to two convents, she was turned down by both because of poor health. The local bishop suggested she take over a badly managed orphanage, the House of Providence. She ran it for six years until the bishop closed it down.

He told the young woman, "You have always wanted to be a missionary. I don't know of any institute of missionary sisters. Why not start one yourself?" So that is what Francesca did. With six girls she had taught in the former orphanage, Francesca founded a new order, the Missionary Sisters of the Sacred Heart.

In 1877, the new sisterhood began work in a small

Franciscan friary in Codogna. Without any resources, the sisters begged for funds to run their convent. By 1880, they received the first official approval of their order from the bishop of Lodi. Not long after, they did so well that they opened a branch in Milan and then Rome. In 1888, the new order won papal approval, and Francesca became known as Mother Cabrini.

In the final years of the nineteenth century, hundreds of thousands of poor Italians immigrated to America, hoping for a better life. They settled in big cities such as New York, Chicago, and Boston, where they lived in crowded, filthy slums. Most Italian immigrants knew no English, and had no training to earn a livelihood. They existed in poverty and misery. Pope Leo XIII was disturbed by the suffering of those Italian immigrants. Recognizing the courage and resourcefulness of Mother Cabrini, he said to her, "Instead of serving as a missionary to China, why not go west to help your fellow Italians in the New World?" The idea appealed to her as worthy work for her missionary order.

Not long after, Mother Cabrini heard from Bishop Michael Corrigan of New York. If her order would come to New York, he had a building he could offer them for a convent and school in the great city. Mother Cabrini was delighted and she and six sisters set sail from Italy, arriving on March 31, 1889.

The building the sisters were offered was not what they had expected. It was old, crumbling, and in poor repair, but the sisters set to work cleaning and scrubbing, preparing the place to minister to the needy Italian immigrants.

In an unbelievably short time, Mother Cabrini opened a chain of convents, schools, orphanages, and hospitals across the United States. In each she sought to serve needy immigrants from her native land. Mother Cabrini often faced opposition from both clergy and laity, who didn't want huge numbers of Italians filling their area. Yet, nothing stopped her. In time, she expanded her work to Central America, Argentina, Brazil, Spain, and even England.

In spite of a lifelong fear of water, this courageous little woman spent months crossing and re-crossing the Atlantic Ocean. Her life became one long series of travels by boat, train, and carriage; she even crossed the Andes Mountains by mule.

In 1892, Mother Cabrini opened the great Columbus

Hospital in New York City, later founding a similar hospital in Chicago, naming both after the Italian discoverer of America.

While working in Seattle in 1909, Mother Cabrini became an American citizen. She had given much to her adopted country, building schools, orphanages, and hospitals. By then her order had grown to a thousand sisters in eight countries.

Mother Cabrini taught her sisters, "Love one another. Sacrifice yourselves for your sisters. Be kind to them, never sharp or harsh. Don't harbor resentments, but be meek and peaceable."

One night, Mother Cabrini dreamed of a large country estate looking over the wide Hudson River. It was a perfect place for children. She told her dream to Bishop Corrigan. He was amazed. It was the exact description of a 450-acre estate on the Hudson River owned by Jesuit priests. He told Mother Cabrini, "I think the Fathers plan to sell their property, as it had no good source of pure water."

Mother Cabrini made a low offer on the property in West Park, New York, which the Jesuits accepted. They even gave her an extended mortgage with low payments.

After praying to God for a source of water, the Blessed Virgin appeared to Mother Cabrini, pointing where to dig a well. Suddenly, a clear mountain spring gushed out of the ground. The problem was solved.

Soon after, several carriages full of orphaned children arrived at the new convent. There they could enjoy clean air far from the city slums. Mother Cabrini enjoyed working with the children. She joined them at games and attended their festivals and performances, but closest to her heart was their care and education.

She instructed her sisters, "My daughters, in your hands lie the next generation. It is your privilege to mold families and society."

The sisters did other work besides caring for children. They cared for families in big-city slums, nursed victims of yellow fever during an epidemic in New Orleans, and descended into Colorado mines to minister to Italian miners.

Because of her great charitable work, people came to admire Mother Cabrini, and no longer held prejudices against her and the Italian sisters.

At fifty, having established the work of her Missionary Sisters of the Sacred Heart, Mother Cabrini still had to find the money to support her network of institutions.

In spite of failing health and her endless travels, Mother Cabrini still brought strength and wisdom to each of the many institutions she had founded. Nothing got her down. When one sister, heavily burdened by the work and responsibility at her orphanage, complained, Mother Cabrini said to her, "Child, do you think you have troubles? I have fifty establishments to care for. Let us abandon ourselves to God. Then our faces will never look strained, but always calm and radiant."

In 1917, the United States entered World War I on the side of the Allies. For the first time, this valiant little nun felt overwhelmed. Patriotic Americans tried to close her institutions, calling them "foreign," as Mother Cabrini and most of her sisters were Italian-born. She even received threatening letters. Many supporters discontinued their donations.

By then, Mother Cabrini was sixty-seven, emaciated, bent over, with trembling hands. On Saturday, December 17, 1917, she was unable to get out of bed. Later she rose and sat in a rocking chair to make her meditation. It was then the end came. She was discovered dead by a sister.

Mother Cabrini was buried at West Park following a solemn requiem Mass in Chicago. Her remains were later transferred to Mother Cabrini High School in Fort Washington, New York, where they still rest.

In 1928, the investigation began into her sanctity. By then her order numbered more than two thousand sisters who ran sixty-seven institutions in eight countries for the Missionary Sisters of the Sacred Heart.

Once the two required miracles were authenticated, Mother Cabrini was beatified by Pope Pius XII on July 7, 1946, in St. Peter's. She was canonized on September 8, 1950, by Pope Pius XII. He declared the Italian nun, "The heavenly patron of all immigrants and displaced persons." Mother Cabrini was the first American citizen to be canonized.

Her feast day is November 13.

St. Katharine Drexel
The Millionaire Nun
1858-1955

Katharine Mary Drexel was born in Philadelphia on November 26, 1858. Her mother, Hannah, died two days later, leaving Katharine and Elizabeth, her older sister, motherless. Their father was Francis Anthony Drexel, the millionaire partner of J.P. Morgan. Lonely after the death of Hannah, Francis Drexel married Emma Bouvier. Later she had a baby, Louise, and raised all three girls.

The Drexels lived in a mansion with many servants, and also owned a country house called St. Michel.

Both of Katharine's parents were devout Catholics. Francis Drexel visited the girls' rooms every night to hear their prayers. Emma Drexel distributed food and clothing to the poor several days a week. When old enough, Katharine helped her stepmother. Francis also donated large sums to build orphanages and missions. Katharine wanted to give her life in service to the needy, but that wasn't the usual course of wealthy young ladies.

Following Katharine's confirmation at twelve, she

was allowed to take communion. Drawn to the Holy Sacrament, she received as often as allowed.

An exciting event in Katharine's teens was her debut into society. The future saint wore an elaborate gown trimmed in lace, while the crowd of guests danced the night away. Katharine, however, felt uneasy about all that money spent on her; she wanted to be a nun and give everything to God.

In 1874, the entire Drexel family sailed to Europe. The high point of Katharine's trip was an audience with Pope Pius IX. The young girl yearned to ask for his advice about her future, but there was only time to kneel and receive his blessing. In Rome, Katharine met a Belgian priest, Father Peter Hylebos. He was visiting the Vatican from his missionary station in America's northwest. He told Katharine about the poor Indian tribes in the state of Washington. The priest sighed, "If only someone would help them." Into Katharine's heart stole the idea of aiding the Indians.

The following year, Francis Drexel took his family out west, traveling in a private railway car. Imagine Katharine's surprise and joy to find Father Hylebos at a small Indian mission in Tacoma, Washington. Seeing the people's plight strengthened Katharine's resolve to help them. Meanwhile, she thought of becoming a nun, but in which order and where?

Then, in 1887, Father Drexel died suddenly of pneumonia. His second wife, Emma, had also passed away. The vast Drexel fortune was left to his three adult daughters. To drown their grief, the girls made a second trip to Europe. This time Katharine was able to speak to the Holy Father and ask his advice about a vocation to the Indians. Pope Leo XIII suggested, "My dear child, as there is at present no order of sisters serving the Indians, why not start one yourself?" At last she realized what her vocation must be. Katharine Drexel would use her millions to benefit Indians and blacks.

At first, the Drexel girls donated huge sums to start an industrial school for orphans, but there was still Katharine's dream of being a nun. She fulfilled it by entering the convent of the Sisters of Mercy in Pittsburgh. On November 7, 1889, all the Drexel aunts, uncles, and cousins traveled in a private train to see Katharine take her vows. Headlines called Katharine Drexel, "The world's richest nun." She received one thousand dollars a day from her trust fund.

Once the heiress (now Sister Mary Katharine) completed her novitiate, she started her own order, known as the Sisters of the Blessed Sacrament. Thirteen young ladies joined her in the endeavor, using the Drexel summer home for their convent. Now she was called Mother Drexel.

At first the sisters' work was with the Indians out west. Mother Drexel traveled constantly (always by the lower coach fare) to establish schools and orphanages, and instructing the Indians in the Catholic faith. The future saint also built schools for blacks all over the United States. She opened Xavier University in New Orleans, still the only black Catholic college in America. Altogether, Mother Drexel gave away twenty million dollars.

Mother Drexel would have continued her wonderful work, but in her seventies she suffered a severe heart attack. For the following twenty years, she lived quietly in retirement at the convent in Bensalem, Pennsylvania. This extraordinary woman, born to wealth, but vowed a nun, died there on March 3, 1955, at the age of ninety-nine.

Her cause for canonization began in 1964. Always admired for her sanctity, Mother Drexel, like all other candidates, needed two miracles.

After Robert Gutherman's hearing was miraculously restored through prayers to Mother Drexel, she was beatified by Pope John Paul II on November 20, 1988. Then came verification of Amy Walls' healing, the second required miracle. Mother Drexel of Philadelphia was declared a saint by Pope John Paul II in St. Peter's Square on October 1, 2000.

Thousands visit St. Katharine Drexel's shrine in the chapel of the Sisters of the Blessed Sacrament. She is the second U.S.-born saint.